# Jim –
## THE NINE LIVES OF A DYSFUNCTIONAL CAT

# Jim —
## THE NINE LIVES OF A DYSFUNCTIONAL CAT

### by Steven Appleby

BLOOMSBURY

In memory of Jim
1985 — 2004

Special thanks to Nicola Sherring for
suggesting Jim do a book

Thanks also to: Nick Battey; Lisa Birdwood; Pete Bishop;
Jonny Boatfield; Adam Boome; Karen Brown; Liz Calder;
Rosemary Davidson; Mary Tomlinson, Gabrielle Walker &
Matt Willis-Jones

First published 2003

This paperback edition published 2005

Copyright STEVEN APPLEBY © 2003
The moral right of the author has been asserted

Bloomsbury Publishing Plc
36 Soho Square, London W1D 3QY

ISBN 0 7475 7406 5

9780747574064

All papers used by Bloomsbury Publishing are natural, recyclable
products made from wood grown in well-managed forests.
The manufacturing processes conform to the environmental regulations of the
country of origin.

Printed in Great Britain by Clays Ltd, St Ives Plc

www.bloomsbury.com/stevenappleby

I am the centre
of the universe.

# AN INTRODUCTION TO JIM

IT IS A DAY LIKE ANY OTHER AND JIM THE CAT
STARES ACROSS THE GARDEN TOWARDS THE
EDGE OF THE WORLD.

THIS IS WHAT HE IS THINKING:

The world exists purely for me.

It is a test.

The world is made up of moving things, stationary things and me.

I must journey through it, learning and acquiring wisdom, until I pass into the next world.

At which point this world will cease to exist!

JIM APPEARS QUITE CONTENT, BUT INSIDE HE
FEELS VAGUELY DISSATISFIED. SOME
UNANSWERED QUESTIONS LURK IN THE
CORNERS OF HIS MIND, REFUSING TO GO AWAY.

Why is there never a place set for me at the dinner table?

Why has no one given me a set of clothes or a pair of pyjamas?

Why don't I have my own room like the other members of my family?

AS USUAL, CONFRONTING THESE THOUGHTS
MAKES JIM FEEL TIRED.
SOON HE FALLS FAST ASLEEP...

9

It is simpler
to be a possession.

JIM

# JIM'S LIVES...

No. 1 ~ SLOTH.

No. 2 ~ LOVE.

No. 3 ~ ENVY.

No. 4 ~ GLUTTONY.

No. 5 ~ VANITY.

No. 6 ~ DISHONESTY.

No. 7 ~ DEBAUCHERY.

No. 8 ~ CONTRITION.

No. 9 ~ STUPIDITY.

# Life no. 1 ~ SLOTH

*In which Jim does absolutely nothing at all.*

HERE WE SEE JUST A FEW OF THE NINETY-NINE
BASIC POSITIONS:

fig a ~ ON THE SOFA.

fig b ~ ON THE CLEAN WASHING.

fig c ~ ON A FLOWER.

fig d ~ WHEREVER YOU ARE ABOUT TO SIT.

fig e ~ IN THE WAY.

fig f ~ BEHIND YOUR HEAD.

Does Jim have fleas at the moment?

*fig g* ~ ON A TEATOWEL.

*fig h* ~ SNUGGLED UP TO THE TEAPOT.

Cosy...

*fig i* ~ IN THE VEGETABLE CUPBOARD.

*fig j* ~ ON ANY ITEM OF CLOTHING LEFT OUT FOR JUST A MINUTE.

My new jumper!

*fig k* ~ IN THE PRAM.

*fig l* ~ SOME OF THE EVIDENCE JIM LEAVES BEHIND.

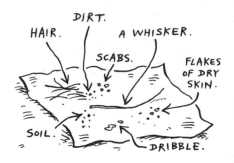

HAIR.

DIRT.

A WHISKER.

SCABS.

FLAKES OF DRY SKIN.

SOIL.

DRIBBLE.

*fig* m — IN THE CHILDREN'S BEDS.

*fig* n — IN YOUR BED.

He *does* have fleas!

*fig* o — ON THE DRAINING BOARD.

*fig* p — ON THE BREAD BOARD.

*fig* q — ON YOUR PILLOW.

*fig* r — ON A CUSHION.

Is he alive?

He hasn't moved at all today.

What's happening? I seem to be having an out-of-cat experience!
FLOAT

17

Look. Jim's fine!
I really thought he'd stopped breathing for a moment there.
miaow...

# Life no. 2 ~ LOVE

In which Jim comes upon the double-edged
sword of LOVE — and cuts himself extremely badly.

Love... Now, THERE'S a worthy calling!
Love is pure...
Mnngh!
Platonic!
Chivalrous...
Hard work!
Yes, I think I'll devote myself to love.
JIM

# LET'S WATCH AND LEARN AS JIM BEGINS HIS QUEST FOR LOVE...

### 1 – RUB AGAINST LEGS.

### 2 – PURR LOUDLY.

### 3 – NUZZLE HAND.

### 4 – LIFT CHIN FOR TICKLING.

### 5 – CLOSE EYES ECSTATICALLY.

### 6 – JUMP ONTO KNEE.

## 7 — PURR LIKE A TRACTOR.

Poo! His breath's a bit strong!

WRRR... WRRR...

## 8 — GAZE UP AFFECTIONATELY.

UGH! There are ghastly knobbly lumps under his fur!

Cysts, I think.

## 9 — CLAW KNEES LOVINGLY.

Anyway, he's SO affectionate, aren't you, Jim? OUCH!

## 10 — CRAWL TOWARDS FACE.

Ah, a lovely cup of tea. Thank you.

## 11 — CLING ON TIGHTLY.

Hop down, Jim, while I drink my tea.

## 12 — DIG CLAWS IN FIRMLY.

I said down. DOWN! Oh, he's up again.

miaow!

Biscuit?

**13 — LET YOURSELF BE STROKED. IT CALMS THEM.**

You're a lovely boy, but enough's enough.

**14 — LOYALLY HEAD-BUTT HAND.**

You've spilt my tea! GET DOWN!

**15 — SHOW THEM YOU CARE.**

He's clinging on gamely... DAMN! He's pulled my jumper!

**16 — MIAOW SEDUCTIVELY.**

Shoo, Jim! Off you go!

**17 — HANG ABOUT WATCHING FOR AN OPENING.**

If you stand up he'll get discouraged and go away.

Good idea.

**18 — NEVER GIVE UP.**

Don't look at him!

**19 — RUN AND JUMP.**

I'll shut him out in the garden. Come on, Jim.

**20 — GAZE BESEECHINGLY TO MAKE THEM OPEN THE DOOR AGAIN.**

He's a super cat, though.

Yes, we all love him dearly.

**THEN SUDDENLY!**

Well, hello... big boy!

Hu... Hu... Hu...

SOON <u>LOVE</u> WAS JOINED BY SEXUAL <u>LUST</u>!

I... I feel a STIRRING down below! A... A HARDENING!!

You're GORGEOUS, baby.

We could have hundreds of lovely KITTENS together, you and I...

Oh, Helen, yes! Yes! LET'S!!

MOMENTS LATER.

I'm not hurting you, am I? I'm rather BIG!

No, you're not hurting me. In fact, you're not doing anything at all!

WHAT?!

I don't understand! It's never happened before... Hang on! There's something missing!

Huh!

<u>I'M</u> going next door. Tiger's still got all <u>HIS</u> bits!

'Bits'?

THE KNOWLEDGE THAT HE HAS BEEN 'DONE' SHOCKS JIM TO THE CORE. HE IS TORTURED BY FEELINGS OF INADEQUACY. DESPERATELY HE TURNS TO HIS FAMILY FOR SUPPORT.

REJECTED, JIM STUMBLES OUTSIDE.

# Life no. 3 — ENVY

In which Jim wants, wants, wants and ends up getting more than he deserves...

Here we go again...

THIS IS WHERE JIM THINKS HE BELONGS
IN THE FAMILY PECKING ORDER:

GET OFF
THE BED,
JIM!

WHERE HE ACTUALLY IS:

31

SOME OF THE HOPES AND DESIRES JIM DREAMS ABOUT:

RESENTFULLY, JIM SETTLES DOWN IN ONE OF HIS FAVOURITE SPOTS FOR A SNOOZE.

Don't dream! What a cheek! In fact, I'm dreaming right now...
z<sup>z</sup>zzz<sup>z</sup>zzzz

Here I am at the controls of the Appleby family estate!

34

35

# Life no. 4 ~ GLUTTONY

*In which Jim becomes just desert.*

JIM CAN'T UNDERSTAND WHY HE ISN'T ALLOWED TO
EAT AT THE TABLE WITH THE REST OF HIS FAMILY.

Their food always
smells more interesting
than mine.

I'll go and get
some human food
elsewhere...

JIM SNEAKS INTO NUMBER
SIXTY-THREE AND STEALS
A STEAK WHICH MRS
BLOATER HAS JUST COOKED
FOR HER HUSBAND'S
SUPPER.

It's ready!

Coming!

THE NEXT MORNING HE
COMES BACK AND STEALS
TWO RASHERS OF BACON
FROM HER FRYING PAN.

OVER THE NEXT WEEK
JIM PINCHES A MEATBALL,
A SLICE OF CAKE, A HAM
SANDWICH, SEVEN CHIPS,
SOME SPAGHETTI AND
A CHICKEN LEG.

JIM WILL
EAT
ANYTHING.

BUT MRS BLOATER HAS
CAUGHT ON...

Enough is
ENOUGH!

I'm going
to put a
stop to all
this
thieving!

Bloody
cat!

SHE TRIES TO FLATTEN
JIM WITH A MALLET.
SHE TRIES TO DROWN
HIM IN THE SINK. SHE
TRIES TO SQUEEZE HIM
BEHIND THE KITCHEN
DOOR. SHE EVEN TRIES
TO SHUT HIM IN THE
FREEZER.

AAARGH!!

AS THE DAYS TURN INTO
WEEKS, MRS BLOATER'S
FURY SMOULDERS INTO
OBSESSION AND THEN
MADNESS.

Grrrr...

Zzzzz

39

EVENTUALLY SHE COMES
UP WITH THE PERFECT
TRAP.

SHE SEASONS A
CHOP WITH
ARSENIC AND
LEAVES IT
SIMMERING ON
THE COOKER
TOP.

TO MAKE SURE NOTHING
SCARES JIM OFF, SHE
GOES OUT TO THE SHOP.

NO SOONER HAS SHE LEFT
THAN JIM JUMPS IN
THROUGH THE OPEN
KITCHEN WINDOW.

UNFORTUNATELY, MR
BLOATER ARRIVES HOME
UNEXPECTEDLY AND
CHASES JIM AWAY WITH
A MOP.

GRRRR...

HE THEN DEVOURS THE
CHOP HIMSELF.

AFTER THE FUNERAL, AT WHICH JIM STOLE SOME PRAWNS, MRS BLOATER RESOLVES TO GET EVEN.

SHE DECIDES TO TRY A DIFFERENT APPROACH.

DAY TWO ~

DAY THREE ~

DAY FOUR ~

DAY FIVE ~

# JIM'S FAVOURITE PLACES TO BE SICK:

### i – ON THE KITCHEN TABLE.

### ii – ON THE COOKERY BOOKS.

### iii – ON A NOVEL, ON SOME CDs OR ON TODAY'S NEWSPAPER.

### iv – IN A DARK CORNER WHERE THE SICK CAN LIE UNDISTURBED FOR WEEKS.

### v – ON THE DOORMAT.

### vi – ON A CHAIR.

NOT FORGETTING: ON THE SWIMMING THINGS; IN A HANDBAG; ON THE BATHMAT; ON YOUR PILLOW; ON SOME UNFINISHED HOMEWORK.

## DAY SIX —

Eat it all or no pudding!

BELCH!

## DAY SEVEN —

Clean your plate, now!

## DAY EIGHT —

Yum yum! Eighty-two beefburgers!

THUD!

TWITCH!

## DAY NINE —

Now it's MY turn!

Cat pie — fair's fair!

Damn! He won't fit in the oven!

43

I'm going to find a
nice quiet garden,
settle down and...

# JIMS FAVOURITE SPOTS TO HAVE A POO:

### i — IN THE FLOWERBED.

### ii — IN THE BARK CHIPPINGS UNDERNEATH THE SWING.

### iii — IN A NEIGHBOUR'S GARDEN.

Ugh!

### iv — IN THE SANDPIT.

### v — ON THE PATH.

Jim's a good cat. He never poos in the house.

Of course not. That's DISGUSTING!

# Life no. 5 — VANITY

In which Jim is dressed to kill... or be killed.

THE CHILDREN KNEW
THAT A CAT WITHOUT A
HAT IS LIKE A YO-YO
WITHOUT STRING.
A POINTLESS THING.

*Cats wear hats.
It says so in a
book.*

*I bet we can find
that poor cat a
hat! I bet we can!*

JIM LAY ON THE WALL
AND STARED ACROSS THE
GARDEN, EYES HALF SHUT,
WATCHING FLIES.

*We'll call you BEAN!
No, SPROUT!*

*No, MR
MACLEAN!*

SUDDENLY...

50

THE DAYS PASS SLOWLY. AND THE NIGHTS...

VERY SLOWLY.

UNTIL...

At last! That was boring.

Ciao, everybody!

# Life no. 6 — DISHONESTY

In which Jim learns to be duplicitous.

SO JIM GOES SNOOPING —
OR RESEARCHING, AS HE
PREFERS TO CALL IT.

HE LEARNS THAT THE
LADY IN NUMBER
SIXTY-SIX TELLS FIBS...

AND THE BOY AT
NUMBER TWENTY-TWO...

AND THE MAN FROM
NUMBER TWELVE.

AND WHEN THE SCRABBLE BOARD COMES OUT AFTER SUPPER THERE IS ANOTHER MESSAGE.

LATER THAT NIGHT...

61

# Life no. 7 — DEBAUCHERY

*In which Tim goes downhill more rapidly than one would believe possible, except in a book.*

I need a stiff drink!

That's what a human would do after a shock like mine, anyway.

LATER.

LATER, IN A DIRTY ALLEYWAY...

EVENTUALLY JIM SOBERS
UP AND STAGGERS HOME.

SHORTLY.

BUT AN HOUR LATER...

IF YOUR CAT DISAPPEARS
FOR DAYS ON END,
READER, BE WARNED!
HE'S PROBABLY ON A
BENDER, LIKE JIM.

We haven't
seen Jim for
days, Mum.

Is he
alright?

Not really,
dear. It's
very
sad.

"So I don't think he's
likely to answer a
prayer for a cat,
do you?"

SLUMP!

"No, Mummy."

"Should we pray for
him, Mummy?"

PATHETIC
CRAWL

"You could try, dear,
but I don't think
it would help. You
see, cats aren't
important to God.
Not like humans."

Then can we get a
new pet?
I'd like
a canary!

Um, we'll see...

I'd like
an elephant!

67

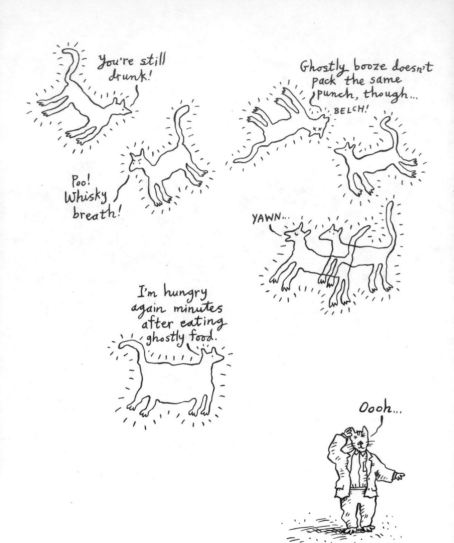

# Life no. 8 — CONTRITION

*In which Jim appears to have learnt his lesson, but...*

72

IN NO
TIME
AT ALL...

74

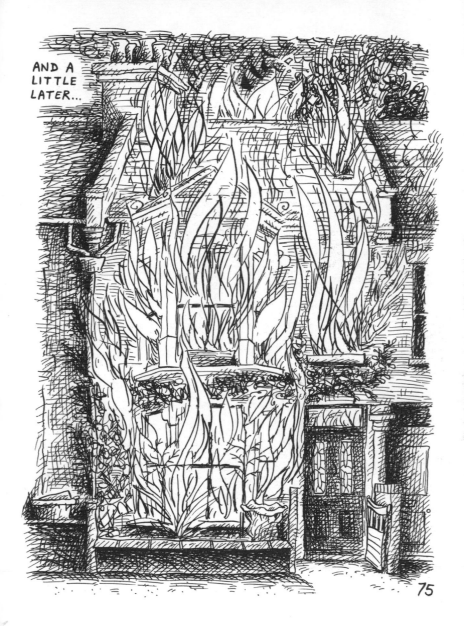

AND A
LITTLE
LATER...

75

# Life no. 9 ~ STUPIDITY

In which Jim completes the test and the world comes to an end...

Jim survived!

HURRAH!

Here I am, back in the good old world, quite content to be a cat and ready to live to a happy old age.

SPLAT!

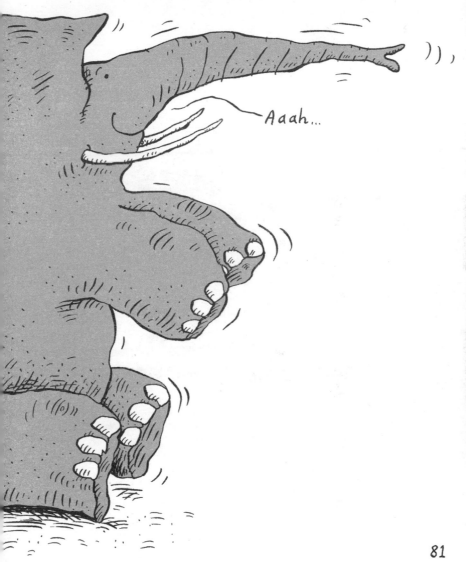

82

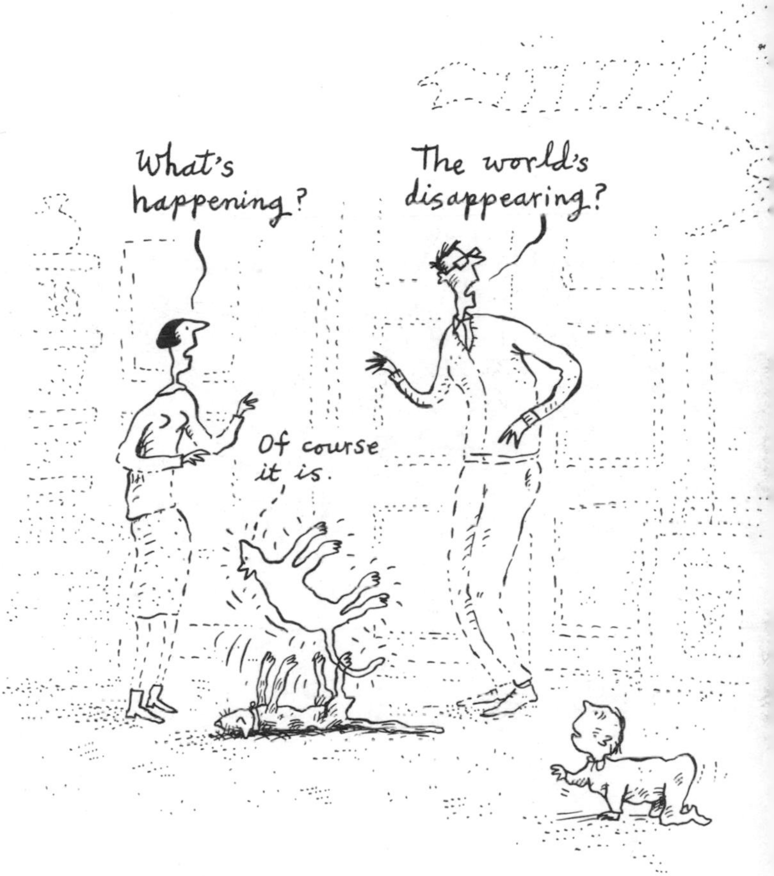
What's happening?
The world's disappearing?
Of course it is.

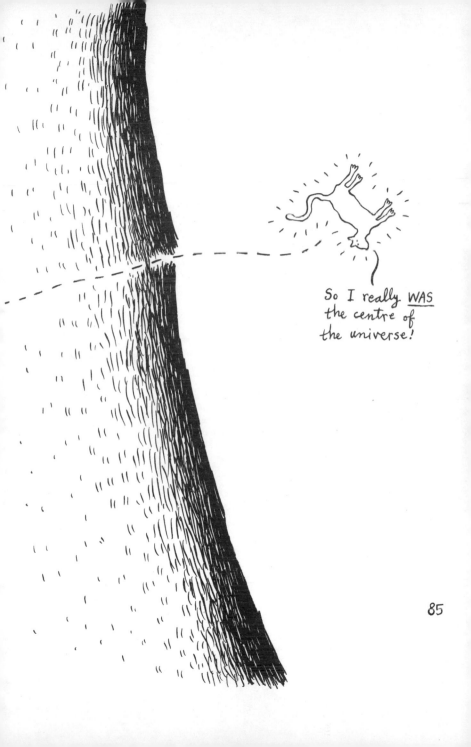

So I really WAS the centre of the universe!

85

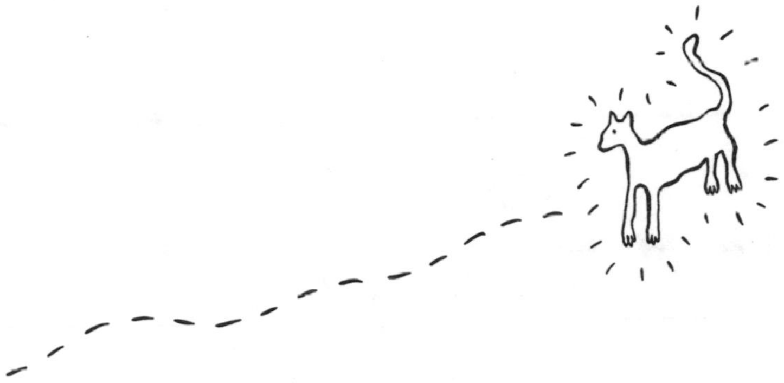

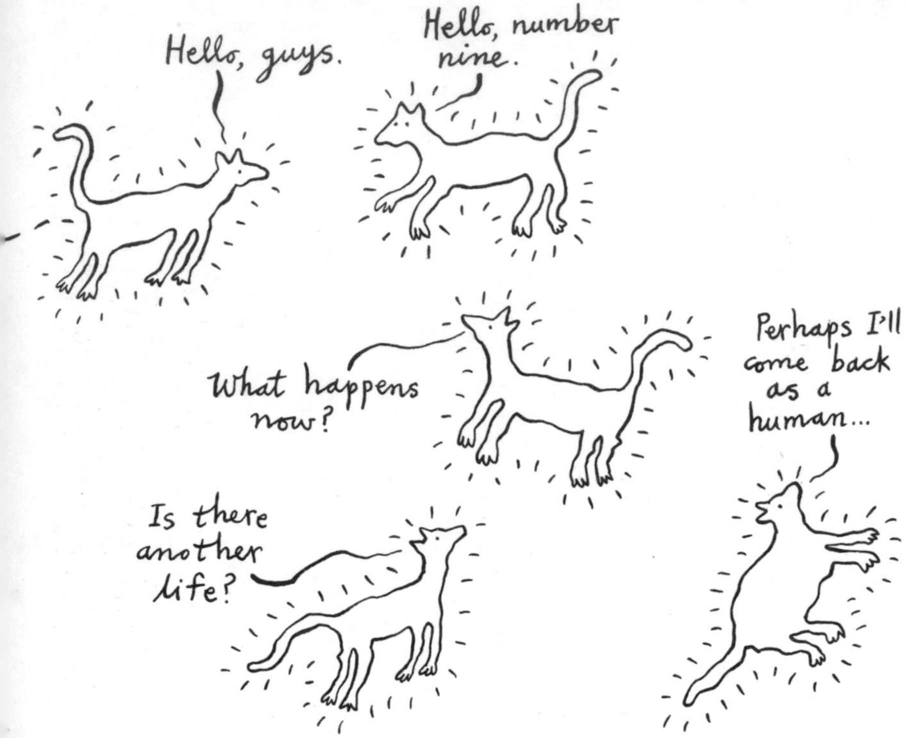
Hello, guys.
Hello, number nine.
What happens now?
Perhaps I'll come back as a human...
Is there another life?

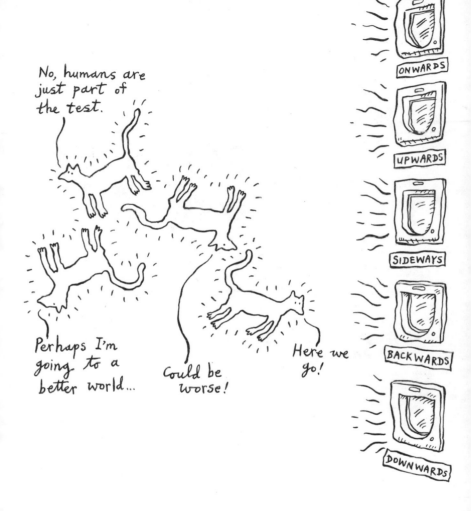

89

The REAL Jim.

The End ?